List of main characters

Brian an Australian Galah from Drop Bear Creek.

Burra a Blue-winged Kookaburra.

Matong a Satin Bowerbird. Matong is an Aboriginal word meaning "strong".

Cinta a Brown Quail. Cinta is a Hindi/Bengali word meaning "worry".

Min a Willie Wagtail. Min is a Chinese word meaning "quick".

Major Mitchell A Major Mitchell Cockatoo and mayor of Drop Bear Creek.

'Have you heard the story about the Drop Bear Creek floods? You haven't? I've told that story a million times. I must say that it's nice to meet someone who hasn't heard that tale yet.'

'It was a pleasure meeting you but I really need to get going.'

'It was back in the summer of 2004 when the trouble began. My mates and I saved the town. It had been raining for several days. Sorry, I've jumped too far ahead. I should start by introducing myself and telling you a bit about my friends. The name's Brian and I come from Drop Bear Creek.'

'Drop Bear Creek is a quaint little town. It's easy to find too if you're keen for a visit. Turn right at Melbourne and head towards Darwin - you can't miss it. It's a peaceful spot and the water in the winding creek is as pure as snow. Not that I've seen snow. The water must be clean because Old Man Platypus is pretty fussy and he only swims in crystal clear water. And the trees - don't get me started on the trees.'

'Well that's good Brian because I really need to fly.'

'Towering river red gums line the banks and there are plenty of nesting hollows if you're looking for a place to stay. You could even stay at my place if you like. And don't forget about the ghost gums - they look beautiful in the moonlight. We've also got loads of scribbly gums. Did I mention the wattle trees?'

'No Brian but you did mention a flood.'

'It was the first day of 2004 - that's the first day in January if you're not too good with maths. My mate Matong is great with his maths. It also happened to be my birthday. Burra woke the whole town up as usual that morning with his dawn chorus. No one knows what Burra is laughing at but I guess everyone's sense of humour is different.'

'I woke up a bit cranky that morning to tell you the truth. I was hoping it would be sunny for my birthday but it was pouring again. Mum told me to cheer up and reminded me that my surprise birthday party was on that afternoon.'

'My surprise party was the worst kept secret in town. Not that we were inviting the whole town because we've only got a small nest. My friend Cinta was coming though which was a big deal because Cinta is often too scared to leave her house.'

'The big moment finally arrived and I entered the living room and expected everyone to shout, "Surprise - Happy Birthday Brian!" Instead, everyone just laughed. I'd put my pants on backwards. I was so embarrassed that I turned pink. Well, pinker than normal. Dad saved the day with one of his jokes.'

'You're a bit of a galah aren't you Brian?'

'Everyone laughed, including me. Well, not quite everyone. My friend Burra just looked puzzled.'

'Brian, I thought you were *all* galah,' he said.

'It's probably a good time to tell you a bit about my
friend Burra. He's a Blue-winged Kookaburra. Burra
doesn't usually understand other birds' jokes. For a
start, he often laughs before you get to the funny bit.
And his laugh - it's like an alarm clock that you have
accidentally set too early. The funny thing is that Burra
doesn't seem to notice that everyone else finds his
laugh annoying. That's one of the reasons Burra finds
it hard to make friends.'

'Dad says that he's surprised we're friends because we are so different from each other. Well, I prefer to think about what Burra and I have in common. We both love sitting in the tree tops, having a chat and watching the world go by. Actually, it was quite brave of Burra to come to my party because he doesn't like crowds and, given I'm so popular, there was quite the crowd at my party. I mean the whole town wasn't there as I said before, but most of the town was. Despite Burra being afraid of crowds, he came to my party anyway because he knew that I wanted him to come. That's what I call a good friend.'

'During the afternoon of my party it continued to rain cats and dogs. Burra of course explained that rain was composed of water, not animals, and that there were no cats and dogs anywhere in sight.'

'Well that's good,' said my friend Cinta, 'because I'm scared of cats and dogs.'

'Let me tell you about my friend Cinta.'

'Cinta is a Brown Quail and she is what my Mum calls,
"anxious". It means she often worries. Sometimes I
worry that my pants are on backwards. But Cinta has
trouble sleeping at night because she is so busy
worrying about things that might go wrong the next
day. She is even scared of heights and spends most of
her time on the ground in the long grass.'

'Mum says she can't believe we're friends because
we're not at all alike. Mum obviously hasn't seen how
much fun we have together in the long grass playing
hide and seek. Cinta was worried about coming to my
party but she came just for me. That's what I call a
good friend.'

'So, the creek was rising Brian?'

'The rain kept getting heavier and Cinta told me at the party that she was *really* worried about the level of Drop Bear Creek. My mate Matong told Cinta that he would check out the creek for her. That's what Matong does - he checks. He can't resist checking on things. He's what my Dad calls, "obsessed." Matong is a Satin Bowerbird. He loves the colour blue. He loves it so much that he built his whole house blue. Matong's house is made of sticks and lots of blue objects and it is called a bower. I must say that his bower is spotless. Matong cleans his house even when it looks perfect.'

'At the party, Matong gave me a present for my birthday. It was wrapped in blue wrapping paper. After I opened my present, he asked me if he could have the wrapping paper back.'

'Well, like Cinta, Matong was also worried about the creek. He kept leaving my party to check the water level. He didn't check just once or twice. He checked every ten minutes. Matong kept leaving the party so often that it started to annoy me. My Uncle Barry said that you could've knocked him over with a feather when he first learnt that we were mates because he thinks we're poles apart. I mean, I can't even check to see if my pants are on the right way. On the other hand, Uncle Barry said I could learn a few things from Matong about how to keep my room tidy.'

'But I like to think that Matong and I share lots of interests. For instance, we both enjoy eating seeds. However, Matong usually counts how many seeds he eats which I think is a bit weird.'

'At my party, when Matong wasn't checking on the creek, he spent his time cleaning up the mess in the kitchen so that I wouldn't have to do it later. Now that's what I call a good friend.'

'Brian, you mentioned that your mates saved the town.'

'Well, I haven't told you about all of my friends yet. You see, I've got this friend called Min. She knows how to liven up a party. Min's a Willie Wagtail and she just can't keep still. She can't even keep her tail still. Min's constantly darting from one place to the next. She finds it a bit hard to pay attention. She doesn't even notice when my pants are on backwards. I had to remind her twice when my surprise birthday party was on. Min was making me a present for my birthday but she didn't quite get it finished.'

'Aunty Beryl was quite taken aback when she found out that Min and I were friends because she reckons we're like chalk and cheese. But Min and I both enjoy playing games together, especially when we should be doing our chores. Actually, Min's very creative and is always making up new games.'

'Despite the rain, Min wanted everyone at the party to have fun. Min organised all the party games and made sure that my birthday was a day that I would never forget. That's what I call a good friend. I wish I had as much energy as Min.'

'So, what happened next?'

'Well, Matong arrived back at the party after checking the creek and remarked that Cinta had good reason to be worried. Burra asked Matong if they could go and look at the creek together. Things must have been serious because Burra and Matong are not the closest of mates. Burra usually feels uncomfortable around Matong. He says that Matong is always staring at his blue feathers and just waiting for one of them to fall out. But both birds are very smart and they respect each other.'

'It just so happens that "attention to detail" is Burra's middle name. Actually, his middle name is Kevin but you get the picture. Unfortunately, Burra often doesn't get it - the big picture that is. However, he does notice the tiniest details about stuff. As they both observed the creek, Burra noticed that the grey rock on the river bank - the one where he had once caught a small snake - was fully under water. Burra noticed that Old Man Platypus was nowhere to be seen. He noticed something else as well. Burra noticed that Drop Bear Creek had turned into a raging river.'

'Just then, my birthday wish came true. The rain stopped and the sun poked its head through the dark clouds. Matong and Burra both looked at each other.'

'We need to evacuate the town,' they both said.

'When Matong and Burra returned to the party, all the guests were heading home. Min had kept everyone entertained and even the adults had enjoyed themselves. Matong saw the mess that had occurred while he was away and started to clean up but Burra said the cleaning up could wait.'

'Brian! Team meeting!' said Burra. 'We need to evacuate. Drop Bear Creek is going to break its banks. The town is going to flood.'

'I put my wing on Burra's shoulder. I told him that the rain had stopped, the sun was out and that everything was going to be okay. That's when Matong and Burra explained why I was wrong. That's when I panicked. That's when Cinta took charge. And that's when my mates and I saved the town.'

'I never thought that Cinta would cope well in an emergency but she knew exactly what to do. Apparently she had been preparing for a flood for years. Cinta had a plan. She also had a plan in case of drought, bushfire, cyclone or blizzard but that's another story.'

'Cinta explained that the first step was to talk to Major Mitchell. Major Mitchell was the Mayor and only he could give the order to evacuate. There was only one problem - he didn't like me. He couldn't even bother showing up to my party. Then again, I didn't invite him but that's no excuse. Major Mitchell didn't seem to like anyone who wasn't a cockatoo. He especially didn't like birds that he thought were a bit strange. Birds that woke you up every morning with their raucous cackle. Birds that worried over nothing and hid in long grass. Birds that were obsessed and built blue houses. Birds that couldn't keep still and pay attention. And particularly birds who didn't know how to put their pants on properly.'

'Major Mitchell was asleep when we arrived. Apparently he was tired because someone had woken him up early that morning.'

'Evacuate!' he screeched. 'Why would we evacuate? I admit that I had my concerns when it rained non-stop all week but, if you haven't noticed you silly birds, it stopped raining an hour ago. The danger has passed. Besides, the creek has never broken its banks.'

'That's when Matong explained to Major Mitchell that it had actually been raining for twenty-one and a half days. When it comes to counting, you don't argue with Matong. He then told the Mayor that since the rain had stopped, the creek had continued to rise exactly twenty-eight centimetres every thirty minutes. Matong had triple checked his calculations. I did tell you earlier that Matong was a whiz at maths.'

'Burra chirped in and added that the creek had indeed broken its banks before - December, 1952 to be exact. Burra amazes me - I can't remember how to put my pants on properly but he remembers just about everything. He told Major Mitchell that if a creek has flooded before, it is capable of flooding again.'

'But it has stopped raining,' said the Mayor. 'Why is the creek still rising?'

'Because north of town are the Wombat Hills,' explained Cinta. 'The rain that has been falling there will eventually make its way to Drop Bear Creek. According to Matong's calculations, the water will keep rising for another thirty-six hours. The problem is, the creek will break its banks in three.'

'No problems,' said Major Mitchell. 'Have you forgotten that we have wings? We'll fly up high into the treetops until the danger has passed.'

'Some of the quails like me are afraid of heights,' said Cinta.

'Then they can escape the flood by going to the Wombat Hills,' said the Mayor. 'The rest of us can perch in the tallest branches and stay in town.'

'But the way to the Wombat Hills is not safe,' said Cinta.

'What about Matong and the other male bowerbirds? They'll lose their homes,' said Min.

'They can rebuild,' said Major Mitchell. 'Anyway, birds of a feather flock together - isn't that right Brian? That's the way it's always been. Parrots look out for their own kind. We don't interfere in the business of others. I suggest the tree dwellers head for the trees and the land lovers head for the hills.'

'That's when I felt sorry for Major Mitchell. He couldn't see that all types of birds have their own particular strengths. He could only see their weaknesses. I looked the Mayor in the eyes and gave him an earful.'

'What did you say to him Brian?'

'I reminded the Mayor that Drop Bear Creek was more than a place on a map - it was a community. I explained that a community looks out for one another, no matter the colour of your feathers or how you flap your wings. I told him the biggest danger facing our town wasn't a flood but what would happen if we failed to help those who needed our help. Not just bowers and nests would be destroyed but our town spirit would be washed away as well. Bowers and nests could be rebuilt, I told him, but rebuilding community spirit wasn't so easy.'

'So, how did Major Mitchell respond to *that* Brian?'

'The Mayor's crest rose to its full height, he stared at me for the longest time, and then he smiled.'

'Brian, you're not such a galah after all.'

'As a matter of fact,' said Burra, 'Brian is a *total* galah.'

'Good one Burra,' said the Mayor, 'but we've no time for jokes. Cinta, tell me about this plan of yours.'

'Burra sounded the warning cry. His high-pitched cackle alerted the town to the danger that was fast approaching. Min did what she always did best - she sprang into action. She darted from home to home, informing all of the Drop Bear Creek residents of the evacuation plan.'

'The Brown Quails were the first to leave. They left the long grass and ran to the Wombat Hills. They were flanked by a squadron of Kookaburras for protection. The parrots, the largest population in Drop Bear Creek, assisted the bowerbirds in dismantling their homes. Poor Matong could hardly bear to watch. Then the creek burst its banks.'

'The water raced towards the parrots and bowerbirds who were frantically working to remove the bowers. As the raging torrent bore down, Brian and the birds grabbed sticks and other objects between their beaks. They launched themselves into the air just as the flood smashed into what was left of the bowerbirds' homes. The parrots and bowerbirds had managed to save most of the materials needed to rebuild the bowers. Every single bird from Drop Bear Creek made it safely to the Wombat Hills. They waited there for two weeks until the floodwaters receded. Most importantly, all the birds of Drop Bear Creek waited together.'

'When it was safe to return to Drop Bear Creek, the birds worked side by side to rebuild their community. Burra helped by making sure everyone got off to an early start each morning. Min's creative ideas and designs were used to build new and improved bowers. However, Min couldn't convince Matong to choose a different colour for his new home. Matong had lost several pieces of blue material from his original bower and he was at a loss.'

'Hope this helps,' said Burra as he plucked a blue feather from his wing and handed it to Matong.

'That's the spirit,' squawked Major Mitchell.

'And that's how we saved Drop Bear Creek. We stopped the floods from washing away the town's spirit. To this day, the birds of Drop Bear Creek continue to care for one another. Old Man Platypus even came back once the creek returned to normal.'

'What an amazing story Brian! Now, I really must fly.'

'Did I ever tell you about the Drop Bear Creek bushfires?'